W9-BBV-053

SPORTS HEROES AND LEGENDS™

JESSE OWENS

Read all of the books in this exciting,
action-packed biography series!

Hank Aaron

Barry Bonds

Joe DiMaggio

Tim Duncan

Dale Earnhardt Jr.

Lou Gehrig

Derek Jeter

Michelle Kwan

Mickey Mantle

Jesse Owens

Ichiro Suzuki

Tiger Woods

Jesse Owens

by Tom Streissguth

Lerner Publications Company/Minneapolis

Lerner Publications Company
A division of Lerner Publishing Group
241 First Avenue North
Minneapolis, MN 55401 U.S.A.

Website address: www.lernerbooks.com

Cover photograph:
© Bettmann/CORBIS

Library of Congress Cataloging-in-Publication Data

Streissguth, Thomas, 1958-
    Jesse Owens / by Tom Streissguth.
        p.   cm. — (Sports heroes and legends)
    Includes bibliographical references and index.
    ISBN-13: 978-0-8225-3070-1 (lib. bdg. : alk. paper)
    ISBN-10: 0-8225-3070-8 (lib. bdg. : alk. paper)
    1. Owens, Jesse, 1913—Juvenile literature. 2. Track and field
athletes—United States—Biography—Juvenile literature. I. Title.
II. Series.
GV697.O9S87 2006
796.2'092—dc22   2004029979

Manufactured in the United States of America
1 2 3 4 5 6 – JR – 11 10 09 08 07 06

Contents

Prologue
Record Breaker
1

Chapter One
Moving North
4

Chapter Two
Racing to Beat Himself
12

Chapter Three
Easy Wins
22

Chapter Four
Buckeye Bullet
30

Chapter Five
Training for Olympic Glory
41

Chapter Six
Victory in Berlin
49

Chapter Seven
Citius, Altius, Fortius
58

Chapter Eight
Banned for Life
66

Chapter Nine
A Wandering Man
78

Chapter Ten
Troubled Times
87

Epilogue
Keeping the Faith
96

Personal Statistics
99

Track-and-Field Records Set by Jesse Owens
100

Sources
102

Bibliography
103

Websites
104

Index
105

Record Breaker

Jesse Owens stood in front of a huge crowd at Stagg Field in Chicago, Illinois. The pressure was on, but he wasn't nervous. The 1933 National Interscholastic Championship meet was under way. The best high school track-and-field athletes from across the country were taking part. Event officials mingled on the field, and reporters scurried from one interview to the next. Track-and-field events were becoming very popular—especially in the Midwest—and some of the biggest newspapers in the country had sent reporters to cover the event.

The families and friends of the athletes had much to see that afternoon, but a great deal of the attention was focused on Jesse. The young, slim African American teenager wore a track-suit from East Technical High School in Cleveland, Ohio. He'd started life as the son of a poor farmer from Alabama, but he was rumored to be the best young track athlete in the country.

Jesse's coach, a slender Irishman named Charles Riley, stood by his side, watching carefully as his star runner went through his warm-up routine.

Jesse was at the end of an outstanding high school athletic career. In his four years of high school, he'd lost only four races. He expected another strong showing in this competition. He moved with ease and confidence—on and off the track. His running style combined grace and power, setting him apart from his competitors, who often struggled and grimaced as they sprinted.

Jesse approached the starting line for the broad jump (later called the long jump). He set his body over the mark, letting his arms dangle loosely from his sides, preparing his legs and feet for the sprint. He took off down the track, planted his foot just behind the foul line, and pushed off with all his strength. He landed 24 feet, 9⅝ inches away, beating his competition easily and setting a new high school record.

He was the clear favorite in the 100-yard dash and didn't disappoint the crowd, tying the world record of 9.4 seconds. That time beat the former high school record by two-tenths of a second and beat the National Interscholastic Championship meet record by three-tenths of a second. And Jesse wasn't finished—his final event was the 220-yard dash. Jesse sprinted around the Stagg Field track at a blistering pace, never letting

2

himself slow as he pulled well ahead of the pack. He put on a burst of speed at the end, leaving the judges shaking their heads in disbelief at the sight on their stopwatches: a new high school record time of 20.7 seconds.

Jesse's incredible performance led East Technical High School to an easy victory. All eyes at Stagg Field were on Jesse as he received the meet trophy, and the crowd exploded with cheers. Jesse Owens had left no doubt that he was the finest high school track athlete in the country. He had been approaching or breaking world records in several events for years—and he was still just warming up.

Chapter One

Moving North

On sultry August days, the wooded hills near Oakville, Alabama, offer shelter from the heat and sun. The hills are a good place to run and explore and to forget for a while the struggles and hard work of the real world. Dirt paths wind around trees and shrubs, small bubbling creeks, and lots of hiding places. With two good legs and a pair of strong lungs, it's easy to escape into the woods for a few hours and take a vacation from everyone else.

> Jesse's first running hero was his father. On Sunday afternoons in Alabama, Henry Owens would race against men from nearby farms. He always won. Henry also taught his son a few leg exercises to help him develop strong muscles.

Somewhere in these hills stood the home of the Owens family, a one-story house made of long wooden planks. The family's ancestors had come to America from Africa as slaves. They took the name of a local landowner named Owens, and they worked the surrounding fields before the Civil War (1861–1865). After the war, they were legally free but had nothing in the world to call their own. Laws and customs prevented most freed slaves from owning any land, getting a decent job, or offering their children more than a basic education.

 During the cotton harvest in Alabama, Jesse had to pick 100 pounds of cotton a day!

By the turn of the twentieth century, life wasn't getting easier. Henry Owens married Mary Emma Fitzgerald (known as Emma) and started a family. Like many other African American families, the Owenses were sharecroppers. They paid the rent for their home by giving half of the crops they grew to the landowner. Henry Owens had the use of the land and a house to live in but few possessions and no money. Day after day, the family struggled to put food on the table and to keep themselves in decent clothing. Summers were hot, and winters brought biting cold, dampness, and rain. The children attended school only when they weren't needed in the fields.

Henry and Emma Owens had nine children before the birth of James Cleveland ("J.C.") Owens on September 12, 1913. J.C. was often sick with colds and other health problems, but the family had no money to pay for doctors. He seemed to get pneumonia (a lung infection) every winter. He was skinny and undernourished, and he suffered from painful boils on his skin. But he had strong legs, and he loved to run. No kid in Oakville could keep up with J.C. whenever he put on a good burst of speed.

HOME REMEDY

When J.C. was five years old, he found a painful bump on his chest. The nearest doctor was seventy-five miles away, so his parents decided they would take care of the problem on their own. His mother heated a knife in the kitchen fireplace to sterilize it before she cut out the boil. J.C. bled for three days afterward, but eventually he healed. Later in life, Jesse said he believed he had nearly bled to death. He credited his family's prayers during those three days with saving him.

Henry Owens accepted the hard life of a sharecropper. He had no ambition to move anywhere else and no thoughts of getting another occupation. But his wife dreamed of a better life, and their daughter Lillie showed the family a way out. Lillie had moved north to Cleveland, Ohio, had found a husband, and was sending letters home describing the big city. She reported that there were factory jobs in Cleveland that paid wages every week. African Americans could find solid homes and apartments to live in and decent schools for kids to attend. In Cleveland a poor sharecropper from Alabama could achieve some independence and put plenty of food on the table.

After reading Lillie's letters, Emma Owens urged her husband to move the family north. Henry was reluctant—farming was all he knew, and there weren't any farms in Cleveland. But he finally gave in. He thought about J.C., his youngest son, who was still in elementary school. In Cleveland, J.C. and his older siblings could get an education and have a chance to raise themselves out of poverty.

---

66 *[J.C. would] run and play like everybody else, but you never could catch him.* 99

—MATTIE TAYLOR, JESSE'S COUSIN

7

At this time, many other African American families in the United States also decided to move north. They left behind familiar homes for strange cities and new jobs at humming factories in cities such as Cleveland, Chicago, and Detroit. In the early 1920s, the Owens family joined this migration, boarding a train for the long ride north. They settled in Cleveland's East Side, home to many other African American families from the south as well as immigrants from Poland and Czechoslovakia who worked in the city's mills and factories.

The move threw J.C. into a strange new environment. Instead of fields and forests, he found sidewalks and street corners. He couldn't run free anymore—cars and people were everywhere. J.C. no longer helped his father at planting and harvest time, so he took an after-school job in a shoe shop to bring a little money into the house. His brothers took part-time jobs as well, while J.C.'s mother and sisters worked as maids and store clerks.

J.C. began at his neighborhood school, Bolton Elementary. He felt a little lost and out of place in the huge city school. Bolton's principal initially placed nine-year-old J.C. in first grade because of his lack of schooling in Alabama. Although J.C. was soon moved to the second grade, his shyness still overcame him at times. On the first day of school, when his teacher asked his name, he murmured, "J.C.," in a thick Alabama accent. His teacher heard "Jesse" and wrote it down that way. From that day forward, J.C. Owens was Jesse Owens.

❝I always loved running. . . . You could go in any direction, fast or slow as you wanted, fighting the wind if you felt like it, seeking out new sights just on the strength of your feet and the courage of your lungs.❞

—JESSE OWENS

Jesse struggled with his reading and math lessons in the classroom. His parents couldn't read or write, so they couldn't help him with his work. But Jesse did well in gym, where he could easily outrun and outwork the other students. On days when the weather was mild, the class went out to the nearby high school track, where Jesse would win short sprints and broad-jumping contests. The legs that had once carried him up and down the rural hills of Alabama made quick work of the flat cinder tracks.

On some days, a short, gray-haired Irishman named Charles Riley watched Jesse's gym class from the sidelines. Riley was a gym teacher and track coach for Fairmount Junior High School. While working at Fairmount, he often came over to watch the kids from Bolton Elementary. Jesse watched Riley too. "I'd noticed him watching me for a year or so," he recalled.

"Especially when we'd play games where there was running or jumping."

He was looking for natural athletic talent, and in Jesse Owens, he realized very quickly that he had found it. Owens was thin, almost scrawny, but he was quick off the starting line and he could run.

TRACK TALK

Cinder tracks were the running surface in Jesse Owens's day. The surfaces were made up of small rocks, carbon, ash, and slag. They were sloppy and slow in rainy weather and slippery in high temperatures. To run at their best on a cinder track, athletes had to use long, heavy, spiked shoes for traction. In modern times, artificial tracks made of rubber and polyurethane have replaced cinder tracks nearly everywhere.

One day Riley approached Jesse and introduced himself. He offered to coach Jesse in the techniques of track-and-field competition and to turn him into an athlete. When Jesse was ready for junior high, Riley told him, he could try out for the track team. Jesse had never dreamed of competing as a track athlete before. He knew only that he loved to run. Charles Riley's challenge opened his eyes to a new opportunity, and he prepared himself to race.

We used to have a lot of fun. We never had any problems. We always ate. The fact that we didn't have steak? Who had steak?

—JESSE OWENS

Chapter | Two

Racing to Beat Himself

The Owens family worked hard in Cleveland. The family earned enough money to afford food and warm clothing for all. They no longer had to fear deadly sicknesses, such as flu and pneumonia, during a cold winter. The family still couldn't afford a car, so they walked or took streetcars to get around town.

> When Jesse first began training with Charles Riley, he coughed a lot during practices. His lungs were still weak from his childhood bouts with pneumonia.

At school and with Coach Riley, Jesse found that track and field was catching on fast. These exciting athletic events were experiencing a huge surge of popularity. The sport appealed to blacks and whites alike. Fans especially loved watching the short sprints of 100 meters (or 100 yards) and 200 meters (or 200 yards). Track athletes also competed in longer sprints, the hurdles, and distance running, such as the marathon, a 26.2-mile race that imitated a run by an ancient Greek messenger. Field events included the broad jump, the high jump, the pole vault, and the discus throw.

A NEW WAY TO START

In the nineteenth century, at the start of the modern track-and-field era, athletes began races standing upright at the starting line, waiting for the sound of the gun. In the late 1800s, an American athlete named Michael Murphy was the first to crouch down at the starting line. At the start of the twentieth century, track sprinters began making starting blocks for themselves by digging out small troughs behind the starting line. They placed their back feet in these holes and pushed off to get a faster start. They also began wearing relatively lightweight leather track shoes for greater speed and traction on the cinder tracks.

High schools and universities across the United States formed track teams that competed in state and national meets. The United States sent a team to the Summer Olympic Games every four years, and the U.S. athletes came to dominate many of the events, especially the short sprints and the broad jump.

Jesse's training with Charles Riley became more serious when Jesse entered Fairmount Junior High. For the easygoing Jesse, intense training meant a new commitment of time and energy. In the Owens house, Jesse was the first to get up in the morning. He arrived at school long before the first bell, making his way to the outdoor track to work out with Riley. Although the track team practiced in the afternoons, Jesse had an after-school job. He couldn't quit his job, so he trained alone with Riley in the mornings.

The workouts began with stretching. Riley had Jesse stretch the calf muscles in his lower legs and the quadriceps muscles in his thighs. Jesse bent his body forward and back, rolled his head from side to side, and did arm circles to limber up his arms and shoulders. These warm-ups made his muscles more flexible and helped prevent injuries such as twisted ankles and sprained knees.

Riley and Jesse met every day on the sidewalk outside Fairmont Junior High for before-school workouts. After Jesse broke his first running record, Riley nicknamed him the "sidewalk champion."

Jesse also worked to achieve intense concentration without tensing his body. Sprinting demands total attention, but it also requires that the body be completely relaxed. Relaxed muscles and joints perform most efficiently, while muscle tension hinders speed and flexibility. It was this ease of movement, partially taught and partially natural, that gave Jesse his advantage on the track.

❝You can teach technique to dash men, which will help them, but, basically, sprinters are born, not made, and Owens was a natural. He had natural speed and a naturally smooth style and he learned form fast. He may have been the most amazing natural athlete ever.❞

—CHARLES RILEY

The morning practices included a lot of work on the most important part of any sprint—the start. Sprinters work carefully on a smooth start, which coordinates the movements of the arms, legs, and torso. This coordination allows the runner to run faster and with less effort. Jesse dug out a small hole in the cinder track. This gave his back foot something to push against so that he could quickly get up to full speed. He carefully placed his hands behind the starting line, with his thumbs and fingers supporting much of his weight. Riley spoke the starter's words:

"On your mark, get set, go!" Jesse pushed hard off his back foot and, to cut wind resistance, kept his body low to the ground for the first few strides. He ran with the lightest-possible steps—as Charles Riley reminded him, he ran as if his feet were touching hot coals. He tried to move faster with every step so that he was still speeding up at the finish line.

> ❝The 100-yard dash is a fast race, not like a horse race where you have a minute or two to spot your leaders and your challengers. . . . Here, you've got to get off with the gun. . . . The runner must know who's in front—whether he's moving more in front—whether anybody has a chance of catching him in those last fifty yards, which fly by in a literal handful of seconds!❞
>
> —JESSE OWENS

For the 200-meter races, Jesse and other runners had to maintain a high rate of speed through a longer period. Running at the same burst of speed needed for the 100 meters was impossible. The 200 meters demanded more stamina than the 100 meters and also careful control of position. Standard tracks are 400 meters all the way around (measured from the inside lane), so the 200-meter sprint is exactly halfway around the track. Since the outside lanes are slightly longer than this distance, the runners line up in staggered positions at the start. Each runner must negotiate two turns in the course of the race. Careful body control is necessary to keep one's balance and run as efficiently as possible around those turns.

In Jesse Owens's time, the 100-yard dash was the most popular sprint in the United States. But meters were used in Europe (and at the Olympic Games), where the metric system had replaced the English system of feet and yards. Since a meter is slightly longer than a yard (1 meter = 1.09361 yards), times were slightly greater for the 100-meter dash.

Like other young athletes, Jesse trained in several different events, including the short sprints, the high jump, and the broad jump. But Jesse was a pure runner, who did best in events that required his top speed over a short distance. He stopped training in the high jump, and although he would later go out for football and basketball, he didn't last long in either sport.

Riley knew that Jesse had the raw athletic ability to succeed. He watched closely every time Jesse ran, paying careful attention to his leg kick, his arm motion, the position of his head, and the look in his eyes. Jesse was easy to coach, but in meets, Riley noticed a bad attitude. Jesse lacked the serious-ness, desire, and determination to defeat his opponents. For Jesse, running was still a game, not a sport. He did it for the sheer joy of running, not for trophies and the applause of a crowd. When he felt confident, he would try to stare down his opponents and intimidate them. At other times, if he fell behind in a race, he would give up and not try his hardest.

BREAKING BARRIERS

In the early 1900s, the top track-and-field athletes were white. But in the 1920s, African Americans began to challenge the color barrier in top-level track competition. Ned Gourdin, an African American athlete from Harvard University, set a new broad jump world record of 25 feet, 3 inches. Gourdin won a silver medal at the 1924 Olympics, but another African American athlete, William DeHart Hubbard, broke Gourdin's mark with a leap of 25 feet, 10⅞ inches. Hubbard also set a new world record of 9.6 seconds in the 100-yard dash.

Riley taught Jesse never to give up on a race, to keep run-ning as fast as he could and then a little faster. He also instructed Jesse to stop trying to intimidate opponents, to keep his eyes forward, and to race with an important goal in mind—faster times. Under Riley's coaching, Jesse learned that a runner must block out his opponents and race against himself. He must focus only on the finish line.

Riley took an interest in Jesse's life off the track as well as his efforts on it. On weekends, the coach would bring Jesse to his house for lunch. He gave Jesse advice on schoolwork and dealing with teachers. He told a lot of stories, but as often as not, he made a point by simply showing Jesse what he meant to say.

One day, Riley drove Jesse to a horse-racing track outside of Cleveland. He had Jesse watch the Thoroughbred horses carefully and told him to pay close attention to their faces. He pointed out that the faces had no expression. The horses didn't play mind games with their opponents—they simply ran as fast as they possibly could. The speed and strength to win, Riley said, came from determination.

Jesse responded to his coach by running smarter and starting to win. He also started breaking records. In 1928 he set a new world record for junior high schoolers in the high jump, at 6 feet, and in the broad jump, at 22 feet, 11¾ inches.

That same year, Riley invited Charley Paddock, the most famous track star of the time, to speak at Fairmount Junior High. A champion sprinter from the University of Southern California, Paddock had won the 100-meter dash and finished in second place in the 200-meters at the 1920 Olympics in Antwerp, Belgium.

The 1920 Antwerp Games

Charley Paddock's 100-meter win at the 1920 Antwerp Games was only the beginning for the U.S. track-and-field team. The team won both first and second place in the 100 meters and the 200 meters. It won the 400-meter relay. It took five of six medals in the two hurdles races and won the 3,000-meter team relay, the high jump, the pole vault, the 56-lb. throw, and the hammer throw. The team won silver medals in the 800 meters, the broad jump, and the steeplechase as well as the pentathlon and the decathlon.

In the 1924 Olympics in Paris, France, he won a silver medal in the 200-meter dash and finished in fifth place in the 100-meters. In both years, Paddock also ran on the gold medal 4×100 relay team. Paddock was known for his unique style of finishing races—if he had a chance of winning, he would leap at the finish tape. He was the first man to run the 200-meters in less than 21 seconds. After Paddock finished speaking, Riley brought him to his office and introduced him to Jesse.

Jesse never forgot that meeting. Confident and enthusiastic, Paddock told stories of competing in front of vast crowds for the most prestigious athletic honors in the world. He spoke well and he dressed well, and Jesse saw in him the possibility of a better life, one in which he wouldn't have to worry about getting enough to eat or finding decent clothes to wear. From that moment on, Jesse began to dream about competing in the Olympic Games.

❝*I knew I was going to the Olympics someday, impossible as it seemed. . . . I unceasingly worked—no, slaved—to become faster and faster, jump farther and farther. . . . The taut tape at the finish line began becoming familiar to me.*❞

—JESSE OWENS

Chapter | Three

Easy Wins

Under Riley's direction, Jesse began consistently winning sprints and broad jump competitions. His family was pleased with his success, but they were still struggling. In 1929 Henry Owens was hit by a taxi while crossing a Cleveland street. He suffered a broken leg and couldn't work for several months. A doctor who examined Henry discovered that he was blind in one eye. This vision problem made him unsuited for factory work.

At about the same time, the country experienced an economic downturn. In October 1929, the stock market crashed. Many companies went bankrupt and had to fire millions of workers. One by one, Jesse's older brothers had to drop out of school and take low-paying jobs to support the family. Several of Jesse's brothers married but, unable to afford homes of their own, they brought their new wives to live in the Owens home.

Games. The 100-meter final went down as one of the most incredible races in Olympic history. Tolan and Metcalfe crossed the line so close together that the timers on the field couldn't agree on a winner. The race judges examined a photograph of the finish closely for several hours before deciding to give the gold medal to Tolan but to make their official times identical, at 10.38 seconds. In the 200-meter dash, Tolan won again, while Metcalfe took a bronze medal for finishing third. Ed Gordon, another African American athlete, won the broad jump gold with a leap of 25 feet, ¾ inch.

The Los Angeles Olympic Games were the first to use automatic timers and photo finishes, in case the finish of a track event was in doubt. They were also the first to use the victory stand and to play the national anthems of the gold medal winners.

That summer, Jesse's disappointment at not making the Olympic squad was mixed with uncertainty in his private life. In August, his longtime girlfriend, Ruth Solomon, gave birth to a baby girl and named her Gloria Shirley. Ruth and Jesse weren't quite ready for parenthood. They were still in high school, and they didn't have a house of their own. They had little money to support any kind of family, and they weren't even married. Ruth and the baby continued living at home with her parents. To make ends meet, Ruth had to drop out of school and take a job in a beauty parlor. Jesse found himself responsible for the care of a second family. He had a lot more on his mind than just running as his senior year at East Technical began.

 Jesse finished first in seventy-five of the seventy-nine races he ran in four years of high school.

Jesse was popular with his classmates. They admired his friendly personality as well as his athletic ability. To Jesse's surprise, they elected him senior class president. Adding to his leadership duties, Jesse was named captain of the East Tech track team.

Jesse continued training hard, and he made sure that he was still the man to beat at track meets. Edgar Weil and Charles Riley had improved his running form so well that Jesse beat his opponents with little effort. His starts were smooth. He held his head steady and he kept his arms close to his body. He stepped lightly on the track, barely touching the ground with his heels before springing off the front of his feet.

At a state meet in Columbus, in May 1933, Jesse set a new high school broad jump record at 24 feet, 3¾ inches. This jump broke the old record by more than 3 inches! Jesse's record-breaking performance at the national high school finals in June at Chicago's Stagg Field was the perfect ending to his outstanding high school career. When Jesse returned home, the city of Cleveland threw him a victory parade. He rode in an open car to city hall, where the mayor and several other local politicians were waiting to congratulate him.

Chapter | Four

Buckeye Bullet

By the time East Technical High School held its graduation ceremony, everybody who had even the slightest interest in track and field knew Jesse Owens's name. More important, track coaches at every university in the country knew who he was. The Big Ten teams—especially the University of Michigan and Ohio State—were inviting him to enroll and join their track teams. At this time, the Big Ten was the most prestigious athletic conference in the country, made up of the schools that all the top high school athletes wanted to attend.

Jesse turned to Coach Riley for advice. The two men drove to Ann Arbor, the home of the University of Michigan, to meet with the coaches there. They also visited Ohio State in Columbus and Indiana University in Bloomington. Jesse considered the advice of Ralph Metcalfe, who recommended his own Marquette University. But Jesse felt a strong loyalty to the state of Ohio, and he wanted to be able to visit his parents, Ruth, and Gloria from time to time. He chose Ohio State.

Jesse's report card posed a serious problem, however. He had never taken much interest in class work. His grades were barely good enough to get him into college, and he still lacked the credits needed to officially graduate from East Tech. To improve the situation, he took a series of entrance exams in the summer of 1933. He passed the tests, and in the fall he moved to Columbus to begin his freshman year.

OHIO STATE BUCKEYES

The "Buckeyes" of Ohio State were named after a poisonous shrub that once grew throughout the state of Ohio. A log cabin made from the timbers of buckeye trees was adopted as an emblem by Ohio resident William Henry Harrison. He ran for president of the United States in the election of 1840. Since that time, the state of Ohio and Ohio State University have had Buckeye as their nickname.

Jesse's family didn't have enough money to pay for college. At this time, schools didn't offer athletic scholarships for track-and-field athletes. In addition, Jesse couldn't accept money for competing for or being a member of the Ohio State team. Doing so would invalidate his status as an amateur athlete—meaning he wouldn't be able to compete in college track meets or in the Olympic Games. Instead, he needed a job. Many athletes worked at their schools' stadiums and training facilities to earn money for tuition and books. Jesse hoped he could also earn enough money to send a little home to his parents and Ruth.

FAMOUS OHIO STATE ATHLETES

- Bob Clotworthy, gold-medal-winning Olympic diver (1956)
- Glenn Davis, winner of three Olympic track-and-field gold medals (1956 and 1960)
- Alice "Lefty" Hohlmayer, original member of the All American Girls Professional Baseball League
- Ford Konno, swimmer who won four Olympic medals (1952 and 1956)
- Jack Nicklaus, professional golfer
- Lea Ann Parsley, Olympic silver medalist, skeleton—a lugelike sport (2002)

Fortunately, Jesse had the help of a Cleveland businessman named Richard Kroesen. Kroesen owned a chain of sporting goods stores and was a big fan. He asked friends in Columbus, the capital of Ohio, to arrange a job for Jesse as an elevator operator in Columbus's capitol building.

With Kroesen's help, Jesse had a way to support himself. But the menial job made him realize that even though he was a track star, he still had serious responsibilities and challenges to deal with in the real world. It also made him hungrier than ever for the kind of success that would free him from poverty.

WEDNESDAYS WITH JESSE

At Ohio State, Jesse took advantage of his spreading fame as a track athlete to give speeches at local schools and in front of social clubs and civic organizations. He spoke about the Ohio State program and about his own experiences in training and competition. Jesse gave the speeches every week, on Wednesdays at noon, and earned $50 for his expenses each time.

Ohio State opened his eyes to another fact of life: racial discrimination. The university was already well known for its racist policies. While Jesse attended the school, only about one hundred of the fourteen thousand students were African American. Ohio State banned African Americans from campus dorms and imposed other rules that separated the races in public places. African Americans were also not allowed in many of the restaurants and movie theaters that surrounded campus.

At the state capitol, Jesse's bosses put him in charge of the freight elevator, at the back of the building, rather than at the passenger elevator, at the front, where white athletes worked. But Jesse strove to make the best of the situation. Fewer people rode the freight elevator, so he had more time for uninterrupted study.

Jesse threw himself into his schoolwork. He chose to major in physical education, and he found his classes to be very challenging. University rules required athletes to maintain a certain grade point average to compete for the school. But Jesse didn't want to risk slowing his progress on the track. He often neglected his books as he worked out alone during the fall, preparing himself for his debut in the spring.

In the spring of 1934, Jesse began training with Larry Snyder, the Ohio State track coach. Snyder found himself dealing with an extremely talented athlete, but he saw room for improvement. Jesse's arms weren't working as hard as they should, in Snyder's opinion, because Jesse was holding them awkwardly high instead of dropping them naturally. Snyder worked hardest on starts, showing Jesse how to close his stance at the starting line to get a more powerful spring off his front foot. Snyder also changed Jesse's broad-jump technique, asking him to churn his legs faster in a "hitch kick" to get more distance in the air.

The results began to show immediately. As a freshman, Jesse couldn't yet compete on the varsity team, but he did take part in exhibitions and open meets in early 1934. He also competed in warm-ups (practice races before the main event) at the Ohio State varsity meets. On May 5, just before the varsity team took the field against Notre Dame, he set three records, one a state mark in the broad jump and the others world record times at 90 and 120 yards. (The time for each distance was clocked during a single run of 120 yards.) That year, even though he wasn't on the Ohio State varsity squad, he was elected to the All-America track-and-field team, a squad of the best athletes in the country selected by the Amateur Athletic Union (AAU).

Traveling to meets, Jesse had to face new forms of racial discrimination. Although he was welcomed at track meets everywhere, he wasn't usually welcomed at hotels and restaurants. When the track team traveled, some restaurants refused to serve the African American members of the team. In those cases, they had to wait for white teammates to bring them food. Some hotels would only allow African Americans as guests if they used the back entrance and rode the freight elevator.

If Jesse experienced bitterness and hatred at this racism, he didn't show it. He avoided fights and confrontations, and he shied away from any situation that he knew might cause problems. Jesse had several white role models in his life, including

Coach Riley and Charley Paddock. He knew from personal experience that blacks and whites could build strong friendships.

> **"**[Charles Riley] was the first white man I really knew, and without ever trying, he proved to me beyond all proof that a white man can understand—and love—[an African American].**"**
>
> —JESSE OWENS

In the spring of 1935, Jesse finally joined the Ohio State varsity track team. He had worked hard with Coach Snyder to perfect his starts, learning to dig in deep and shorten his stance. The quicker starts helped him to demolish the Big Ten competition. At his first Big Ten meet, at Indiana University, he won three races and took second place in the 70-yard high hurdles. But Jesse knew that his real opponents were the world record times in the short sprints and the runners who would be trying out for the Olympic team of 1936.

The road to the Summer Olympic Games wasn't always smooth. That spring, Jesse suffered a back injury that caused him nagging pain and discomfort. He could only relieve the pain with hot baths, rubdowns, and heat pads. On May 25, 1935, by the time of the National Collegiate Track and Field Championships, he was still hurting. But once Jesse reached the field, warmed up, and started running, the pain disappeared.

At the championships, held in Ann Arbor, Michigan, the coaches were still uncertain whether or not to let Jesse run. As he warmed up on the sidelines, Jesse talked fast to convince them his back was strong enough. Although they were doubtful, they allowed him a start in the 100 yard dash. Jesse promised that if he felt any pain after that race, he would drop out of his other events. Jesse simply blew away the competition, running the short sprint in 9.4 seconds, tying the same world record he had tied at Stagg Field in 1933.

❝[Owens] blazed down the turf runway... with every ounce of his amazing speed, struck the take-off squarely and rocketed off into space. Before he landed it was apparent that he had achieved the record.❞

—ASSOCIATED PRESS

Next came the broad jump. With his victory in the first sprint, Jesse was feeling bold. He measured out the world record distance, at 26 feet, 2½ inches, and set down a white handkerchief at the mark. He pulled himself up at the start, his eyes intent on the takeoff line and the handkerchief lying beyond. He rushed to the line and took off with a strong push, working his legs and arms furiously and landing well beyond the white handkerchief. The jump inspired Jesse to a running, dancing leap of joy as the judges stretched out the measuring tape to an incredible 26 feet, 8¼ inches—a new world record by nearly half a foot.

With Charles Riley watching from the stands, Jesse prepared for the 220-yard dash. After trying and setting world records in his first two events, Jesse wasn't going to let his coaches stop him from running again. He didn't disappoint them, setting a new world record in the 220-yard dash, running in 20.3 seconds. (The former record had been held by Nebraska native Roland Locke since 1924.) Jesse finished off his remarkable day by running the 220-yard low hurdles in a world-record-setting 22.6 seconds. Jesse's incredible performances at the Ann Arbor meet made him one of the best-known athletes in the nation and in the world. Newspaper reporters dubbed him the "world's fastest human" and spread his name, his picture, and his story across their pages.

After the Ann Arbor meet, Jesse's teammates elected him team captain. This was the first time an African American was captain of any athletic team in the Big Ten.

That summer Jesse traveled to California with the Ohio State track team. He won all four of his events against the University of Southern California, a top track team coached by Dean Cromwell. Jesse won again at the National Collegiate Athletic Association (NCAA) championships, held in Berkeley, California, the home of one campus of the University of California. After this meet, the team traveled to San Diego, where Jesse beat an up-and-coming sprinter named Eulace Peacock in the 100-meter dash and the broad jump. In the last ten events he had competed in, Jesse had won every single one.

Jesse found himself the focus of stadium crowds, newspaper reporters, and flocks of young women who wanted to shake his hand and have his autograph. But when Ruth Solomon, back in Ohio with their child, heard about the situation, she became very upset. She heard rumors that Jesse was attending wild parties, meeting adoring fans, and staying out late. She knew that Jesse must be facing a lot of temptations, and she worried that he might forget about her. When she heard that Jesse had been seen with a glamorous young woman named Quincella Nickerson, she finally decided to put her foot down. She sent Jesse an angry letter and told him that this was his last chance to marry her.

Worried and a little embarrassed, Jesse prepared for the long train trip back home. But he still had one more meet to attend. He felt distracted, unable to concentrate on his training or on the competition. At the meet in Lincoln, Nebraska, Jesse was beaten in two events by Eulace Peacock. When he arrived home, he found Ruth waiting for him.

Jesse applied for a marriage license that same day. Even though the laws of Ohio said the couple would have to wait five days, Ruth would wait no longer. The couple received special permission from a judge to skip the waiting period. That same evening, July 5, Jesse Owens and Ruth Solomon were married in the living room of the Solomon home. The couple had no time for a honeymoon, but Ruth didn't mind. She knew Jesse needed every moment he could get to prepare for the Olympic trials.

Chapter | Five

Training for Olympic Glory

J esse Owens had become Ohio's star athlete. In the summer of 1935, a Cleveland politician named Dan Duffey helped to arrange a new job for him. He was to serve as a page in the state legislature in Ohio. The job was an easy one. Jesse helped the politicians in Columbus by carrying papers and messages at their request. He earned $21 every week, even in the summer, when the legislature wasn't in session. For the summer, Jesse's job title was "honorary page" since it required no work.

The honorary job as page didn't sit very well with the Amateur Athletic Union, the organization that oversaw college athletics. The AAU learned about Jesse's job and saw it as an athletic scholarship, a gift that Jesse wasn't entitled to as an amateur athlete. In the fall of 1935, the AAU threatened to strip Jesse of his amateur status, making it impossible for him to take part in the Olympic Games.

Jesse had to appear before a committee of AAU officials and explain himself. The committee listened to Jesse say that he hadn't meant to break any rules. His coaches from Ohio State spoke up for him as well. Finally the AAU decided to drop its charges against him. Jesse returned the $159 he had earned that summer.

Jesse planned to spend the fall training for the 1936 Olympic trials. A controversy was brewing, however, over whether the United States should take part in these games at all. Berlin, Germany, had been selected to host the 1936 Summer Games.

❝[Ohio State coach Larry Snyder] was constantly on me about the job I was to do and the responsibility that I had upon the campus. And how I must be able to carry myself because people were looking . . . Everybody's eyes were upon you. And they would scrutinize everything that you did and so you had to be very careful of the things that you did.❞

—JESSE OWENS

Adolf Hitler and the National Socialist (Nazi) Party had recently come to power in Germany. Hitler had fought for the German army in World War I, and he was furious that France, Russia, Britain, and the United States had defeated Germany.

When he took office, he ordered new laws against Jews, whom he blamed for Germany's defeat in World War I. By the summer of 1936, German Jews were being robbed of their money and property, arrested, and forced into exile. Jewish athletes were prohibited from participating in any organized athletics, and they were banned from the German Olympic team.

"The time and place for the Olympic Games of 1936 were fixed by the international committee long before the present German government came into power. . . . [Organized amateur sport] cannot . . . with good grace or propriety interfere in the internal political, religious, or racial affairs of any country or group."

—AVERY BRUNDAGE, JUNE 1935

The choice of Germany as the host of the Olympic Games had become a problem. Many people in the United States and in the rest of the world asked their Olympic teams not to take part. The AAU supported a boycott of the games. Although Jesse took no interest in politics, he was still the best-known runner in the country. He found himself in the middle of this controversy. Reporters sought him out, pressuring him to take a position on the possible boycott.

Jesse was training hard for his chance at Olympic glory. Many African American athletes didn't believe the United States should boycott the games. African Americans experienced racial discrimination every day. Why should the United States have the right to protest the same thing in a foreign country? The head of the U.S. Olympic Committee, Avery Brundage, visited Europe in 1935 to view conditions for himself. The German government showed Brundage the positive side of Nazi Germany—the humming economy, the scrubbed and orderly streets, and the prosperity of a country that had once been mired in economic depression. Nazi officials also explained Germany's thorough preparations for the Olympic Games.

OLYMPIC OATH

Since the Antwerp Summer Games of 1920, the opening ceremony of all Olympic Games has included the Olympic Oath. The modern version of the oath is as follows: "In the name of all competitors, I promise that we shall take part in these Olympic Games, respecting and abiding by the rules which govern them, committing ourselves to a sport without doping and without drugs, in the true spirit of sportsmanship, for the glory of sport and the honor of our teams."

When Brundage came home, he announced that he was dead set against any boycott. His arguments finally prevailed. In December 1935, the AAU announced that it was against an Olympic boycott.

Just when Jesse learned that the United States would take part in the games, he received a piece of bad news. His grades for the fall term were poor, and he'd failed a psychology course outright. He was ineligible for the winter indoor track season. He'd only be able to compete in the spring outdoor season if he got his grades up. Without taking part in collegiate competition, Jesse would have little chance of being in top form for the Olympic trials in late spring.

Jesse wasn't speedy just on the track. In 1936 he was given a speeding ticket while he was driving home to Cleveland for a weekend visit!

Jesse studied hard during the winter months, and he got his grades up enough to get him back on the track team. Eulace Peacock was shaping up as Jesse's top competition for the spring. Peacock was taller and heavier than Jesse, and he had more sheer muscle power in his legs. The two men had emerged as the fastest runners in the country, and their races always made headlines in newspaper sports pages. They had also become close friends. At the 50-yard dash during one indoor meet in Cleveland, Peacock lost his balance at the start. The rest of the runners sped down the track, unaware of what had happened. Jesse won the race, but when he found out about Peacock's troubles, he demanded that the race be run again. On the second try, Peacock beat Owens by a fraction of a second.

EULACE PEACOCK

Eulace Peacock was an Alabama native who, like Jesse, had moved north with his family in search of decent jobs and a better life. In high school, he had competed in football as well as track and had planned to do the same in college. But when Peacock joined the track team at Temple University in Philadelphia, his coach gave him a clear choice: track and field or football, not both. Peacock chose track and soon became one of the best college sprinters in the country. His style differed from Jesse's. Instead of moving with a smooth, graceful motion, he ran with brute strength, kicking hard, working his arms, and plunging at the finish line.

At the Penn Relays in April, Eulace Peacock lined up for the anchor (final) leg of the 400-meter relay. Running all out, he pushed and stretched his right leg too hard and tore a muscle, the hamstring, just before the finish. The injury put him out of action, while Jesse won the 100-meter dash and the broad jump and helped his four-man team win the 400-meter relay.

Eulace Peacock's injury prevented him from training for several weeks. When he returned to the track, his right leg remained weak, and he'd lost much of his running and jumping strength. While Peacock continued therapy for his leg injury, Jesse reached the top of his form, running even faster and stronger. He broke his own world record in the 100-yard dash on May 16 at the University of Wisconsin, setting a mark of 9.3 seconds. At the Big Ten finals on his home track in Columbus, he won all four events that he entered—the 100-yard dash, 200-yard dash, broad jump, and hurdles.

66 *Ralph [Metcalfe] was tall, yet powerful, with legs longer and more heavily muscled than mine, a chest with more lung capacity.* 99

—JESSE OWENS

The Olympic tryouts began just after the college track season ended. This time around, no one could intimidate Jesse. He traveled to Chicago for the regional competition, where he easily qualified for the semifinals in Princeton, New Jersey, on July 4. At the semis, Jesse beat Metcalfe in the 100-meter dash and Peacock in the broad jump.

In 1936 Jesse joined the largest African American contingent in Olympic history. It included ten men (including Ralph Metcalfe and Eddie Tolan) and two women in track and field, five boxers, and two weight lifters.

The finals took place the following week at Randall's Island, New York, where Jesse won the 100-meter and 200-meter dashes as well as the broad jump. Peacock was still hindered by his injury, and he didn't make the Olympic team.

In top form, feeling confident and strong, Jesse was among the most promising athletes to head for Germany. On July 15, just three days after the Olympic tryouts ended, the team boarded the SS *Manhattan* in New York Harbor for the voyage across the Atlantic.

Chapter | Six

Victory in Berlin

The ship carrying the U.S. Olympic team took nine days to cross the Atlantic Ocean and reach Germany. During that time, the country's top athletes ate, slept, walked around the decks, and did very little else. Some suffered from the waves and the rolling of the ship, getting seasick whenever the weather got rough. Out of boredom, others spent too much time at the dining table. With no good way to exercise, they ate themselves out of shape and landed in Europe unprepared for Olympic competition.

At the end of the SS *Manhattan*'s voyage to Germany, Jesse's U.S. teammates voted him the best-dressed athlete on the ship!

Jesse Owens didn't eat a lot. He felt queasy and seasick much of the time. When the ship finally arrived in the port of Bremerhaven on July 24, he was tired, and his legs and body felt stiff from the many days of confinement. He and the other athletes immediately boarded an express train to Berlin.

Germany had prepared the most elaborate Olympic Games in history. Adolf Hitler knew that this was his nation's moment to shine, and he made the most of it. He ordered the capital to be put in thorough order, with all anti-Semitic symbols and signs cleared away. The only symbol to remain was the swastika, the double cross that symbolized the Nazi Party and the new Germany.

The Nazi regime glorified German athletes and often vilified Jews, who were subject to harsh laws, arrest, and seizure of their stores, homes, and property. German athletic clubs banned Jews from membership, and Jews couldn't even train or compete in public venues or swimming pools.

Swastikas hung from banners and flagpoles everywhere, appeared on the uniforms of political leaders and military men, and decorated the halls and stadiums of the Olympic Games. Germany had built an Olympic Village on the outskirts of Berlin to house the male athletes. (The women were housed in a dormitory near the Olympic stadium.) The athletes stayed in small, tidy bungalows. They had the use of parks, forests, and an artificial lake. There were tracks for training and plenty of space to roam, far from the curious crowds of downtown Berlin.

The Germans hadn't posted any sort of security guards around the Olympic Village, however. Anyone who wanted to visit the athletes could walk right in. This situation posed an unexpected challenge for Jesse. To Jesse's surprise, he was already well known in Berlin as the top American runner. People from around the world wanted to meet him. Other athletes, as well as sports reporters and German citizens, came to his bungalow to greet him, shake his hand, take his picture, and ask for his autograph. One morning he woke up to find people snapping photos of him through the window! Jesse did his best to be gracious. His kindness had another unintended effect. His friendly, easygoing manner seemed to attract even more people.

The Olympic Games originated in ancient Greece in 776 B.C. From time to time, the cities of Greece waged war on one another, but according to tradition, all fighting ceased for the duration of the games.

The crowds made Jesse realize that he was one of the stars of the Olympic Games. As an African American, he was also a figure of curiosity. For several years, Adolf Hitler and the Nazi Party had declared that Germans and other white people of northern Europe were smarter and stronger than other races around the world. They looked down on non-Europeans, especially those with dark skin. These ideas weren't confined to Germany. Many people around the world, and even writers and scientists in the United States, shared them. With his world records and his reputation as one of the best runners in the world, Jesse challenged these notions. The Olympic track events were the stage not only for Jesse's quest for Olympic gold but also for Nazi Germany to prove its ideas—or see them proved wrong.

Dean Cromwell, one of the track team's official coaches, and Larry Snyder took charge of Jesse's training in Berlin. Jesse worked for several days to get rid of his wobbly "sea legs" and prepare for competition.

On August 1, the Berlin Olympic Games officially opened. The huge Olympic stadium was packed with 110,000 spectators. Athletes paraded around the track and took their places on the infield. The giant airship *Hindenburg* flew overhead while music filled the air and Olympic and German flags flapped in the breeze. Adolf Hitler gave a short speech, announcing the opening of the games. The Olympic flame was lit at one end of the stadium, and a great flock of doves was released to symbolize the Olympic spirit of peace and friendly competition.

The *Hindenburg* was a German airship, a lighter-than-air craft filled with hydrogen gas. This airship made thirty-six transatlantic flights in the early 1930s before it burst into flames and crashed during a landing approach on May 6, 1937, at Lakehurst, New Jersey.

German athletes began winning on the first afternoon of events. In front of loudly cheering crowds, Tilly Fleischer won the gold medal in the women's javelin, and Hans Woellke won gold in the men's shot put. Both gold medal winners were invited to Adolf Hitler's box to receive personal congratulations. Later in the day, the United States had its first victory when Cornelius Johnson, an African American, won the high jump event with an Olympic record of 6 feet, 8 inches. Instead of congratulating the winner, Hitler left the stadium. Hitler's bad manners angered many reporters from the United States, who wrote that the German leader was intentionally snubbing American winners—including Jesse Owens. Later that day, the head of the International Olympic Committee, Henri de Baillet-Latour, sent a stern message to Hitler.

He must congratulate all the winners, no matter their nationality or color, or none of them at all. From that time on, Hitler didn't offer personal congratulations to any athlete.

On August 2, Jesse took the field for his first event, the quarterfinal heat of the 100-meter dash. He was relaxed and ready, wearing a new pair of athletic shoes his coach had bought him in a Berlin store.

NEW SHOES

Jesse's coach bought him shoes made by Dassler Schuhfabrik, the company that produced the first track shoes that had spikes on the bottom. These shoes gave runners more traction on the soft tracks used in Owens's time. Adolph "Adi" Dassler, the son of a German cobbler, ran the company with his brother Rudi. The Dassler company later split into two shoe companies, Adidas (from *Adi Dassler*) and Puma.

In his quarterfinal run, Jesse tied the world record of 10.3 seconds. That afternoon, in the semifinals, Jesse broke the record at 10.2 seconds. When the judges measured the wind, however, they rejected the record. For world record measurements, the wind was always considered. A strong tailwind pushing the runner forward gave him an unfair advantage and, according to tradition, disallowed any claim of a world record time. But Jesse had easily qualified for the finals, along with two other Americans, Ralph Metcalfe and Frank Wykoff.

Jesse was just as popular with the crowd on the track as he was off the track. Snyder had warned Jesse that the German fans might not be happy to see an African American succeed. He said, "Don't let anything you hear from the stands upset you. Ignore the insults and you'll be all right." Fortunately, the warning turned out to be unnecessary. Jesse received hearty applause after his quarterfinal sprint, and when he stepped on the track before every subsequent event, the crowd cheered enthusiastically.

Coach Larry Snyder wasn't officially on the U.S. Olympic team in 1936, but he worked with Jesse and with high jumper Dave Albritton. Snyder worked hard to correct what he saw as the bad running form Jesse had picked up from his regular Olympic coach, Lawson Robertson.

The 100-meter finals took place on the afternoon of August 3. Six of the world's best runners lined up, stretching their legs with their eyes on the finish line. The runners drew numbered straws for lane placement, and Jesse drew the inside lane—a lane softened up and slow from the morning rain and from events that had taken place earlier. Because the inside lane was so soft, the judges moved all the runners over one lane to the right, keeping the inside lane empty. Along with the other runners, Jesse used a small garden trowel to dig out a place for his feet behind the starting line.

The starter spoke, raising the gun. The crowd grew silent. The gun fired, and Jesse took off smoothly. He ran with the pack for about 30 meters, then began to pull ahead. While the other runners churned and struggled, Jesse moved his legs and arms with ease, like a gazelle bounding down the soggy lane, far ahead of the pack. Near the finish, Ralph Metcalfe began gaining on him. Metcalfe's strong finishes nearly always brought him to victory, but not this time. Jesse was the clear winner, tying the world record again at 10.3 seconds, followed by Metcalfe in second and Martin Osendarp of the Netherlands in third.

❝Owens won today because he is in truth the world's fastest human. No one ever ran a more perfect race. His start was perfect, his in-between perfect, and his finish perfect. The Buckeye Bullet ripped out of his starting holes as though slung by a giant catapult.❞
—ARTHUR J. DALEY IN THE NEW YORK TIMES

After the race, Jesse took the victory stand. A gold medal was placed around his neck, and the band played "The Star-Spangled Banner," the national anthem of the United States. Shortly after the race, he gave a brief radio interview to a reporter broadcasting back home. Jesse's family and the rest of the country were all eager to hear from the Olympic champion. On this day, the United States found a new hero, and Jesse Owens finally achieved his dream.

Chapter Seven

Citius, Altius, Fortius

Jesse didn't have much time to savor his first taste of Olympic gold. He had to compete in the preliminaries for the 200-meter dash and the broad jump on the very next day, August 4. In his two qualifying runs in the 200 meters, he finished with identical times, setting a new world record at 21.1 seconds.

He had a little more trouble in the broad jump. Each athlete had three attempts to qualify for the finals. The qualifying distance was 23 feet, 5 inches, a mark that Jesse had beaten while he was still in high school.

The Olympic motto *Citius, Altius, Fortius* is a Latin phrase that translates into English as "Faster, Higher, Stronger."

The Owens family lived in this house in Cleveland, Ohio. On the porch sit Jesse's two sisters, two nieces, his mother, and his brother.

Jesse's coach, Charles Riley, helped him improve his running form in the 100- and 200-yard sprints.

In this 1933 photo, Jesse, a senior at East Technical High School, shows off his broad-jumping prowess.

Running for Ohio State, Jesse pulls off another seemingly effortless win in the 220-yard low hurdles at a meet in Chicago.

Eulace Peacock *(right)*, a sprinter and broad jumper from Temple University, was one of Jesse's toughest opponents in 1935 and 1936.

Even while traveling to the 1936 Olympics aboard the SS *Manhattan,* Jesse found a spot to practice his jumping skills.

Jesse *(center)* salutes during the presentation of his gold medal for the broad jump. Silver medalist Luz Long *(right)* and bronze medalist Naoto Tajima *(left)* share the podium with him.

Jesse's family gathers in Cleveland, Ohio, on August 6, 1936, to celebrate his three Olympic gold medals. Jesse won his fourth gold two days later in the 400-meter relay.

On June 19, 1948, Jesse raced a horse named The Ocean at a track in San Mateo, California. He wasn't proud that he raced against horses, but he did it to earn money to support his family.

After Jesse's running career came to an end, he enjoyed giving advice to a new generation of African American athletes.

When Jesse ran once through the broad jump track and into the sandpit, just to warm up, the judge raised his red flag, signifying that he had just taken one of his official tries and fouled. This type of warm-up was common in U.S. competitions, but the German judge may not have been familiar with it. On Jesse's second try, he jumped far—but he'd taken off past the foul line, a straight line marked in chalk that an athlete's feet must not touch or cross before the jump. The judge raised his red flag once again.

With only one try remaining, Jesse was on the brink of disqualifying himself. He strolled back to the starting point, trying to relax and focus. He began running, watching the foul line carefully. Just to be safe, he took off several inches behind the line. He threw himself into the air and leaped beyond the 25-foot mark. He was in!

In the broad jump finals that afternoon, Jesse's toughest competition came from Luz Long, a young German athlete. Long was tall, blond, and energetic, matching the Nordic ideal of Nazi Germany. In the eyes of many, the head-to-head duel in the broad jump pit symbolized much more than athletic ability. It became a contest of Hitler's ideas of racial purity against the democratic ideals of the United States.

Jesse had a good first leap of 25 feet, 9¾ inches. But Long matched that mark on his second jump. Jesse pounded down the runway for his second jump, flying past 26 feet. Long couldn't match Jesse in his final jump and had to settle for second place. But Jesse, who had already secured the gold, still had one jump to go. Jesse held nothing back and exploded across the sandy pit, soaring well past his earlier two jumps and setting an Olympic record of 26 feet, 5¼ inches. Long hurried over to Jesse to congratulate him on his second gold medal. After the medal ceremony, the two athletes marched off the field together, talking as friends. That evening they would spend several hours together, discussing their athletic careers and their post-Olympic plans. Although Jesse didn't meet Long again after the Olympic Games, he would never forget the German friend he made at the broad jump pit.

After the 1936 Olympics, Luz Long joined the German army. He sent Jesse several letters during World War II. He was killed in battle in 1939. But Jesse Owens stayed in touch with the Long family. He met Long's son, Karl, in Berlin a few years after the war ended, in 1951.

On the morning of August 5, Jesse competed in the semifinal heat for the 200-meter dash. He won his heat with a time of

21.3 seconds. Teammate Mack Robinson, running in a different heat that morning, matched the 21.1-second record Jesse had set the day before.

The 200-meter finals were unexpectedly delayed by another event. As the runners prepared to take their marks, Harold Whitlock of Great Britain entered the stadium. He was the leader in the 50,000-meter walk, a race that ended with a lap inside the stadium. Whitlock finished the thirty-one-mile race in slightly more than four-and-a-half hours.

Mack Robinson was the older brother of a rising young athlete named Jackie Robinson. Jackie would later be the first African American to play major league baseball.

That afternoon, Owens and Robinson took their marks for the final. The field was muddy from a morning rain, and the air was cool. Jesse had trouble getting his body completely loose and warmed up. All of the runners struggled as the damp weather soaked their shoes in rain, making them heavier and more cumbersome. But when the gun sounded, Jesse burst from the starting line and barreled down the track, leaving Robinson and the rest of the field well behind him. He hit the finish line in a time of 20.7 seconds, beating Eddie Tolan's old Olympic record by a full half second.

At the medal ceremony, the crowd cheered long and loud for Jesse. Jesse felt a powerful sense of accomplishment and satisfaction. He planned to spend the next several days sitting in the stands and cheering on the U.S. team.

The U.S. track coaches still had plenty of work to do. The 4×100-meter relay was coming up, and they had to select the four runners for the team. At the trials in the United States, the coaches had announced a plan to use the four men finishing from fourth to seventh place in the 100-meter dash. This group included two Jewish athletes, Sam Stoller, a runner from the University of Michigan, and Marty Glickman, from Syracuse University in New York.

On the morning of August 8, the day of the race, Coach Lawson Robertson announced that Jesse Owens and Ralph Metcalfe would run the relay with Foy Draper and Frank Wykoff. Stoller and Glickman would have to watch from the sidelines.

The decision threw the entire track team into turmoil. Even though Owens and Metcalfe were running well and winning medals, kicking Stoller and Glickman off the relay team seemed unfair. Worse, it appeared that the U.S. coaches were worried about offending Adolf Hitler. Hitler's hatred of Jews was well known to everyone.

After winning his third gold medal, Jesse took a day to relax and observe other track-and-field events. Even though the sky was filled with dark clouds, he wore sunglasses to avoid attention from the crowd.

Coach Robertson claimed the decision had nothing to do with Hitler. The German squad, he explained, was preparing to run with new sprinters, strong athletes who had been kept quietly off the track and out of the races until now. He had to counter with the best runners on the team, and the best runners were Owens and Metcalfe. Owens and Metcalfe would be able to build such a lead in the first half of the race that the other teams would have no chance of catching up. The explanation didn't sit well with Stoller and Glickman, both of whom had run trial heats faster than Foy Draper. The two men voiced their anger, claiming that any American team would win the race easily. But the coach wouldn't be moved.

Whatever Jesse's opinion of the controversy, he knew he had to obey his coaches. Jesse dutifully put on his tracksuit and his running shoes to squeeze in a few practices before the first heat. The coaches had Jesse run first so he wouldn't have to catch the baton. Jesse practiced running into the changeover zone, carefully bringing the baton up to the next runner's hand smoothly and making sure the baton didn't fall to the ground. It wasn't as easy as it looked—running at full speed made it difficult to keep the hands steady, even for a split second.

In 1998 the U.S. Olympic Committee publicly apologized for its decision to replace Sam Stoller and Marty Glickman on the 4 x 100-meter relay team.

In the morning trials, the U.S. team blazed past the competition, matching the Olympic record of 39.9 seconds. In the afternoon finals, they broke the record by one-tenth of a second. Jesse had no trouble passing the baton, and his burst of speed in first position gave the relay team an immediate advantage. By the time the anchor runner, Frank Wykoff, crossed the finish line, the team was 15 yards ahead of second-place Germany. Jesse Owens had earned his fourth gold medal and set his fourth Olympic record. Although the relay team chose him to stand on the highest step of the victory platform, Jesse graciously gave his place to his teammate and friend Ralph Metcalfe.

After two weeks, the Berlin Olympics drew to a close. Jesse Owens had emerged as one of the heroes of these games, but Germany had triumphed as well. The German Olympic team had dominated its competition outside of the track-and-field events, and it ranked first in total medals, with thirty-three golds and eighty-nine total medals. The United States finished second, with twenty-four golds and fifty-six total. Hungary rounded out the top three, with ten golds and sixteen total medals.

Earlier track-and-field athletes to win three or more gold medals in a single Olympics included long-distance runners Paavo Nurmi and Ville Ritola, both of Finland. In the 1924 Olympic Games, Nurmi won five medals and Ritola won four. Nurmi's speed earned him the nickname "the Flying Finn."

Chapter | Eight

Banned for Life

By the end of the Berlin Olympics, Jesse Owens was a household name in the United States. Everyone knew who he was, and everyone was intensely proud of his accomplishments on the track. The country also took satisfaction that Jesse's wins showed up Adolf Hitler's theories of race superiority—even though Germany had won more medals than any other participating country.

In the meantime, Jesse was eager to return home to celebrate with his family. But his Olympic honors caused an unexpected change in his schedule. The AAU had scheduled several show races across Europe for Jesse and his teammates. Jesse found himself traveling from one city to the next to show off his running and jumping abilities. Still tired from the intense training and preparation for the games, he boarded trains for Cologne, Germany, and then Prague, the capital of

Czechoslovakia, then back to the German town of Bochum. He then took a flight to London. Everywhere he went, he had to meet important people, sign hundreds of autographs, run in short sprints, give interviews to newspaper and radio reporters, and pose for countless photographers. He grew tired, and the constant stress and strain hurt his times and distances. In Cologne, he long-jumped 24 feet, 4½ inches, well short of his Olympic mark, and in Prague, he didn't make 24 feet in the long jump and ran the 100 meters in a mediocre 10.7 seconds.

Despite his fame, Jesse still had no fortune. The AAU earned money from the exhibitions to cover its expenses from transporting the athletes to and from the Olympics. It didn't pay the athletes for their performances on the track night after night. The Olympic stars were given only a tiny amount of spending money. They couldn't go out at night, they couldn't buy any souvenirs, and they couldn't travel anywhere on their own.

The situation made Jesse angry. He realized that the AAU was benefiting from his talent and long years of hard work while he was missing a golden opportunity back home. Finally, in London, he rebelled. At a press conference, he announced that he would return to the United States immediately. He purposely missed a scheduled flight to Sweden and boarded the passenger ship *Queen Mary* with Coach Snyder for the trip back home. Snyder was equally upset with the AAU. He said the organization was treating the athletes like "trained seals." The AAU saw its athletes as valuable property, to be used whenever possible to earn accolades and glory, to raise money, and to promote the AAU. When Jesse Owens dropped out of the AAU-sponsored tour without permission, he made AAU officials furious. While his ship was sailing back to the United States, officials decided to ban him from any AAU-sponsored competition—for life.

The AAU ban meant Jesse's career as an amateur runner was over. If he returned to college, he wouldn't be able to compete, nor could he take part in any more Olympics. Since there were no professional track teams, he would have to find new ways to support himself. And the Depression made such opportunities few and far between. Yet for most Americans, Jesse was still a star. He felt confident that the popularity he had won in Berlin would carry him through and make the AAU ban unimportant.

❝*As governor of Ohio it is my pleasure to convey to you the congratulations of the people of your state for your brilliant achievements in the Olympic Games.*❞
—MARTIN L. DAVEY, GOVERNOR OF OHIO

Jesse arrived back in Cleveland in late August. The city welcomed him with a noisy parade through the downtown streets, followed by a speech delivered by the mayor at the steps of city hall. Next, the capital city of Columbus, Ohio, threw a big parade, in which Jesse accepted the personal congratulations of the mayor of Columbus and the governor of Ohio. When the rest of the U.S. track team arrived in New York City, Jesse traveled there to greet them and to enjoy another parade honoring the athletes.

Looking for a good story, the newspapers were still making much out of the "snub" of Jesse Owens and the rest of the U.S. athletes by Adolf Hitler. Jesse didn't pay much heed to the racism of Hitler or of Nazi Germany, but he did feel snubbed back in the United States. President Franklin Roosevelt didn't even send a telegram or letter of congratulations to Owens. Roosevelt may have been afraid of angering southern voters who didn't believe an African American man—any African American man—had a place in the White House, even as a guest of honor. Jesse had been dealing with similar attitudes for his entire life. He didn't allow them to bother him.

Jesse had reached a crossroads in his life. He was still young and healthy and still the fastest man in the world. The AAU had banned him from amateur racing, but he had already achieved the top honors in that field with his four Olympic gold medals. And amateur racing earned him nothing. The time had come, he realized, to use his ability and his fame to support himself.

Offers came pouring in from radio stations, from Hollywood studios, from jazz bands, and from companies that wanted to use his name to sell their products. Wilberforce University offered him a steady job as a track coach once he finished his final year of college. A popular radio host, Eddie Cantor, offered him $40,000 to appear onstage and on the radio with him for ten weeks. Another famous performer, Bill "Bojangles" Robinson, offered to coach Jesse to dance, sing, and speak in front of an audience. Feeling a little bewildered, Jesse hired an agent, Marty Forkins, to read the offers and negotiate the contracts.

❝ *I'm burned out, I'm busted, and I'm tired of being treated like cattle. I know how hard it is for a member of my race to make money and earn financial security and I have to reach for it while it's being offered me.* ❞

—JESSE OWENS

That fall Jesse also joined the Republican Party for the presidential campaign. He hadn't taken much of an interest in politics previously, but perhaps his displeasure with Roosevelt, a Democrat, had an effect. The Republican Party supported Alf Landon, and they paid Jesse to speak in support of their candidate. The Republicans, the party of Abraham Lincoln, had long been the favorite party for African Americans. But times had changed, and many African American voters changed their allegiance to support the Democratic Party, which had a reputation for helping ordinary workers. For several weeks, Jesse traveled around the United States, speaking to crowds and supporting Landon. He couldn't change the Democratic tide among African Americans, however. Landon lost the election by a wide margin.

BACKWARD BILL

Bill "Bojangles" Robinson was a famous dancer and comedian who performed onstage and in movies. His show business agent was Marty Forkins, whom Jesse Owens also employed after the Berlin Olympics. Robinson claimed some athletic feats of his own—including the world record time of 8.2 seconds for the 75-yard backward dash.

At the same time, Forkins was on the telephone, speaking to promoters, directors, agents, and managers. And day after day, the offers came and went. Many of them vanished completely, turning out to be just rumors or an attempt to get some free publicity. But some were genuine. In the fall of 1936, Jesse earned money by speaking at banquets, doing radio ads, and endorsing products. He also appeared at running exhibitions. The exhibitions took place at fairs, at public celebrations, and at minor league baseball games. Jesse raced against the best runner in town. He usually gave him a good head start and typically won with a comfortable lead. Audiences enjoyed having a chance to see a world-class athlete perform in their town. But Jesse was not truly challenged by these contests.

Forkins arranged these exhibitions and appearances, always looking for something spectacular that would keep Jesse in the newspapers. He found one such opportunity in Havana, Cuba, at the end of 1936. He arranged for Jesse to race the best runner in Cuba, Conrado Rodriques. But when the AAU got wind of the event, the organization threatened to bar Rodriques from any amateur competition in the United States. The Cuban runner pulled out, but Forkins had another race up his sleeve. At halftime of a soccer game, Jesse lined up forty yards ahead of a Thoroughbred racehorse named Julio McCaw. The head start gave Jesse just enough of an edge to beat out the horse and earn $2,000 in prize money.

The race against Julio McCaw wasn't the proudest moment of Jesse's athletic career. He was glad to earn the money, but he wasn't happy to be shown off racing against a horse, as if he were some kind of circus exhibition. All his training and work, the many years of victories on high school and college tracks, and his wins at the Berlin Olympics had brought nothing more than a little bit of money earned from a few silly running exhibitions.

At the time, Jesse didn't see a good alternative to doing the exhibitions. He had to earn a living, and he had no college degree that would help him land a good-paying job. But the speeches and endorsements that Forkins arranged for him were bringing their rewards. The money he earned allowed him to buy a house for his parents and another for Ruth and their daughter. He also bought a beautiful, shiny black 1936 Buick automobile, new clothes, and furniture for the house, and even a car for Charles Riley, his first track coach. In the fall of 1936, after so many years of striving and poverty, Jesse finally felt like a success.

AAU SNUB

The AAU awards the Sullivan Trophy each year to the country's outstanding amateur athlete. But after Jesse defied the AAU and dropped out of the post-Olympic track-and-field tour, AAU officials decided that he no longer qualified for the award. The 1936 Sullivan Trophy went instead to Glenn Morris, winner of the Olympic decathlon.

Jesse wanted to find some kind of steady job, something that would pay him every week. In January 1937, he accepted an offer from Consolidated Artists to appear as a front man for a traveling dance band. The band performed live, and their concerts were also broadcast each week on the radio. Jesse's job was to stand up in front of the band, make a few jokes, speak to the audience, and announce the name of each song.

At first, Jesse enjoyed the spotlight. Soon, however, the tour also showed him the dark side of the music business. The band spent long hours on the road and stayed in run-down hotels. Managers and promoters sometimes cheated them out of their money. The boredom of going through the same routines and hearing the same music night after night began to wear Jesse down. He loved to move and travel and push himself at a hard pace, but he was no musician or singer. He was merely there for his name and his Olympic wins, and he again began to feel like a circus exhibition.

 In the fall of 1937, Ruth gave birth to a second daughter, Beverly.

By April Jesse had had enough of the music business, and he quit the band. In the fall, he formed a basketball team, nicknamed the Olympians. He picked the squad from Cleveland's best basketball players. Several other such exhibition clubs, such as the Harlem Globetrotters, were also touring the country at that time. Like the Globetrotters, the Olympians played against college teams and amateur club teams, and they won nearly every game they played. At halftime, Jesse entertained the crowd by talking about his Olympic experiences and demonstrating running techniques.

The Olympians traveled from town to town by bus and train, collecting a percentage of the money earned from ticket sales. On some nights, good crowds turned out. On nights with bad weather or in towns with little interest in basketball, the team didn't earn enough to pay their expenses. Jesse had a hard time keeping track of the money, and he spent it too easily. Then Jesse's old enemy—the AAU—resurfaced.

 The Olympians won 136 out of 142 games.

When the AAU heard about the Olympians, the organization called Jesse in to question him about the money the team was making. If they made more than their "necessary expenses," then they would no longer qualify as an amateur sporting club. Jesse did his best to explain to the AAU that he wasn't trying to make more money than absolutely necessary. Not satisfied, the AAU suspended the amateur status of the Olympians, meaning the teams that played against them also could land in trouble with the AAU. This also meant no more matches against college teams or against any team wanting to keep its amateur status.

The Olympians were one of the most successful basketball clubs in the country, winning more than ninety-five percent of their games, but Jesse had to break them up after less than a year of play.

Jesse didn't give up on the sports exhibition business. In the summer of 1938, he formed an exhibition softball squad and called it the Olympics. At the same time, he looked for regular work in Cleveland. He took a summer job as a playground director and formed a dry-cleaning business, the Jesse Owens Dry Cleaning Company. His name was still well known, and he felt sure that customers would flock to his business to have their clothes taken care of by the "world's fastest human."

But Jesse had a talent for spending as well as running. With good money coming in from his exhibitions, he had been unable to save anything, instead spending everything he earned on new homes, good clothes, and nice cars—luxuries he didn't have as a child. But he soon found out that he wasn't made for the day-to-day problems and details of managing a business. Often on the road for softball games, he couldn't keep an eye on the store, and the Jesse Owens Dry Cleaning Company closed its doors for good the next year.

The failed business venture landed Jesse in deep debt for the loans he had taken to start the business. He also found himself in trouble with the U.S. government, which billed him for taxes he owed on money earned from exhibition races. The government put a claim on his house in Cleveland as he struggled to come up with the extra money. He got the Olympians back together for a winter basketball tour in late 1938. But he was facing several debts he still couldn't pay and a tax bill from the U.S. government. In May 1939, one month after the birth of his third daughter, Marlene, he had to declare himself bankrupt.

Chapter Nine

A Wandering Man

By 1939 the Berlin Olympics and Jesse Owens's four gold medals were fading from people's memories. Unrest in Europe dominated the headlines. After the Olympics, Hitler had built up a huge army and had ordered the occupation of Austria and Czechoslovakia. He declared that both of those countries were part of the expanding German empire, which he called the Third Reich. He then invaded Poland, touching off World War II in September of that year.

The beginning of World War II brought about the end of the 1940 Olympic Games. The games were supposed to be held in Tokyo, Japan, but in the spring of 1940 Japan—which allied itself with Hitler's Germany— invaded various countries in Asia.

Jesse moved aimlessly from job to job. The traveling and exhibitions were wearing him out, and regular jobs were leaving him broke and discouraged. The amateur baseball and softball teams kept him moving and in front of appreciative crowds, but these teams caused problems of their own. He was no longer running as fast or jumping as far as he could in college. He'd passed his peak.

The answer to his problems, he finally decided, was his education. After leaving Ohio State at the end of his junior year for the Olympics, Jesse had never returned to college. Every year since his return from Berlin, he had made the decision to go back to school, but for one reason or another, he hadn't kept this commitment. Finally he decided to make good on the promise he had been making to himself. He would finish his college degree.

The family moved to Columbus that summer, and Jesse eagerly returned to class. Professors and fellow students recognized him instantly, and they treated him as a star. Jesse opened another dry-cleaning store to earn some extra money, and Coach Snyder hired him to help out with the track team. The eager Ohio State runners listened to his instruction, but the course work wasn't quite so easy. Jesse found himself unable to concentrate in the classroom and unable to work his way through the difficult college-level work. He was also distracted by the demands of the outside world, including the deaths of his parents. Henry Owens suffered a heart attack in the fall of 1940. Jesse came to his father's bedside and watched him pass away.

Although his teachers admired Jesse's achievements on the running track, they were unable to cut him a break with their grades. He was expelled for bad grades late in the fall but then allowed to try once again. Jesse could manage only a 1.07 grade point average and dropped out for good in December 1941.

Shortly before Jesse left Ohio State, Japan staged a surprise attack on a military base in Pearl Harbor, in the Hawaiian Islands. The attack dragged the United States into World War II. Thousands of young men were drafted to join the fight. Jesse had a family to care for, so he was exempt from the draft, but he found another way to help his country. The Office of Civilian Defense asked him to take charge of a national fitness program for African Americans. In this job, Jesse traveled from town to town to hold fitness clinics and to encourage his audiences to support the war effort.

❝ *Being in motion—moving—was always what made me tick. It's what made running so natural to me, those long hours and years of practice you have to put in. . . . I hated to sit or to stand still.* ❞

—JESSE OWENS

The job gave Jesse the satisfaction of working hard for a good cause. Although racism still existed throughout the country, World War II was a time when African Americans found themselves more widely accepted into mainstream American society. African American workers found good-paying jobs in factories, and African American citizens served their country in military units, even though the units were still segregated from whites.

In April 1943, Jesse was ready for a change. He took a job with the Ford Motor Company in Detroit, Michigan. Ford and other U.S. automakers were producing tanks, planes, guns, and spare parts for the war. Ford hired many African Americans to help in the factories. Jesse was to work as assistant personnel director for African American workers. He was in charge of hiring new employees, firing incompetent ones, and settling minor disputes between employees and management. He soon rose to the position of personnel director, with even more responsibility.

Jesse enjoyed the part of his job that allowed him to help workers. "It was a big job," Jesse later wrote. "It also turned out to be a rewarding one. Not many [African Americans] had been hired for jobs in the auto plants before that, and it was up to me to pick the right ones, not only so they'd get along with the whites but so that we'd all get the job done and win the war."

But he didn't enjoy the endless office politics. He didn't get along with top managers at Ford who saw their factories as moneymaking assets and their employees as costly burdens. When World War II ended in 1945, Jesse was fired.

Jesse took this opportunity to set out on the road once again. He traveled with teams such as the Harlem Globetrotters and the Cincinnati Crescents, a baseball club. He suited up in his track gear and dashed across the basketball court or down the baselines. The crowds cheered him on, watching the same perfect form he had showed at his Olympic races. Jesse still ran well, although he was ten years older and a few steps slower.

The 1948 Olympics

In 1948 the Olympic Games took place in London, England. It was the first time the games had been held since 1936. A number of countries—including Burma, Ceylon, Colombia, Guatemala, Lebanon, Panama, Puerto Rico, Syria, and Venezuela—sent athletes for the first time. Japan, Germany, and the Soviet Union did not send teams to participate. The United States won more medals than any other country, with thirty-eight gold, twenty-seven silver, and nineteen bronze.

In 1949 the Owens family moved from Detroit to Chicago. Jesse still received many invitations to show off his running ability or speak to schools, civic groups, and businesses. The jobs and engagements took Jesse away from his family. He spent days and weeks on the road, flying here and there, spending many of his nights in lonely hotel rooms. At home, his three daughters often missed him. But their father loved to be in motion at all times. He loved the sensation of being in a hurry, being faster than anyone else.

In 1950 the Associated Press selected Jesse Owens as the greatest track athlete of the past fifty years. A huge banquet was held in his honor.

People all over Chicago knew that Jesse Owens lived in their town. They looked to him as an example for the rest of the community, in particular, for the African American community. Chicago needed such an example, and Jesse was proud to provide it by giving others the inspiration and guidance they needed. All he had to do was tell his own life story, describe his childhood in Alabama, his struggles in Cleveland, and the incredible hard work he put in to become a champion athlete. He sometimes called himself a "professional good example."

Jesse's days as an exhibition runner ended in the early 1950s. His last show took place in the summer of 1952, at Yankee Stadium in New York City. Between two games of a double-header, he went into his crouch at home plate and, at the starting gun, took off up the first base line. He was trying for the all-time record in running the bases, 13.3 seconds. Nearly forty years old, he ran with grace and ease. Although he missed the baserunning record, he could still make sprinting look effortless.

THE SOVIET UNION

The 1952 Olympic Games were the first in which the Soviet Union fielded a team. The Soviet government, then a strong rival of the United States, saw its Olympic team as a reflection of its own strength and the virtue of its Communist system. For this reason, the Soviet government supported its Olympic athletes with money, housing, and all the time and equipment they needed to train. This new Soviet-style method of preparing for the games was soon copied by other Communist nations in Eastern Europe, and for the next several Olympics, the accomplishments of the Eastern bloc teams equaled or surpassed those of the United States.

Harrison Dillard

Just as Charley Paddock had inspired Jesse Owens, Jesse Owens inspired a young Cleveland hurdler named Harrison Dillard. Dillard was ten years younger than Jesse. After seeing Jesse on newsreel film, Dillard was inspired to train for Olympic glory of his own. Jesse even met his young admirer and presented him with a pair of his track shoes. Between May 1947 and June 1948, Dillard won eighty-two sprint and hurdle races in a row. Although he failed to qualify for the Olympic hurdles in 1948, he won the 100 meters that year in London in the same time as Jesse Owens—10.3 seconds. In 1952, at the Helsinki Games, he finally took gold in the 110-meter hurdles.

Jesse put his love of travel to the test in 1955, when the U.S. government asked him to serve as a goodwill ambassador for the country. He accepted the challenge happily. His job was to fly to foreign countries, meet the people and leaders of those countries, and create goodwill for the United States. At the time, the United States and the Soviet Union were superpower rivals for the support of smaller countries. Jesse's fame as an Olympic runner became a valuable weapon in this "Cold War." In the Philippines, India, and Malaya, he spoke about the bright side of life in the United States—the liberty to live and work as one pleased, the opportunity to succeed, and the chance for prosperity and security.

When Jesse returned to Chicago, he won an appointment as head of the Illinois Youth Commission. He organized athletic contests and training camps for young people in trouble with the law. Jesse saw participation in sports as one of the best ways to fight juvenile delinquency. "Since the war ended, the United States seemed to have experienced an athletic boom," he noted. "Sports like golf, tennis, and bowling were growing fast. . . . Most of all, things were being done in track and field that had never been done before." He believed the athlete's self-respect and sense of fair play and the drive to do his or her best would give many young people the help they needed to straighten out their lives.

Chapter | Ten

Troubled Times

In 1956 Jesse Owens was delighted to receive an invitation to the Summer Olympic Games that year in Melbourne, Australia. President Dwight Eisenhower asked him to attend as his personal representative. The games took place against a troubled background of political tension around the world. The Cold War between the United States and the Soviet Union had split the world into two hostile camps: pro-Soviet governments and those allied with the United States. Several countries boycotted the games for political reasons.

At Melbourne Jesse saw that the world's track athletes were rapidly catching up to him. Cinder tracks had been replaced by smoother surfaces made from asphalt. New track shoes made of synthetic rubber and vinyl, rather than leather, gave the ankles more support, allowing athletes to sprint harder over long distances. The runners also had the use of starting blocks. The U.S. men's track team scored fifteen gold medal victories at Melbourne, besting the rest of the world in the short sprints, the decathlon, and field events such as the discus, the pole vault, and the shot put. The men won medal sweeps (gold, silver, and bronze all going to U.S. athletes) in the 200-meter dash, the 110-meter hurdles, the 400-meter hurdles, and the discus throw. American women won gold in the high jump (Mildred McDaniel) and silver in the long jump (Willye White).

In 1975 the last of Jesse's world records fell when Alabama native Cliff Outlin ran the 60-meter dash in 6.4 seconds, beating Jesse's forty-year-old mark of 6.6 seconds.

Jesse looked on with a sense of pride, but he also felt a bit of regret. The star of the track-and-field competition that year was a tall, twenty-one-year-old Texan named Bobby Morrow, who grew up idolizing Jesse Owens and dreaming of matching his hero's Olympic victories. Morrow won the 100-meter and 200-meter dashes, becoming the first athlete to win both events since Jesse had done it at the 1936 Olympics. For good measure, he broke Jesse's 200-meter record of 20.7 seconds by one-tenth of a second, winning the race by more than a yard. Morrow's 4×100-meter relay team also won gold and broke the 1936 record of 39.8 seconds by three-tenths of a second.

Four years later, Jesse's last remaining Olympic record fell. The broad jump had been renamed the long jump. Ralph Boston long-jumped 26 feet, 11¾ inches, while trying out for the 1960 Olympic team. Jesse's old record was 26 feet, 8¾ inches. At the Summer Games that year in Rome, Italy, Boston won the event with a jump of 26 feet, 7¾ inches.

One of the most exciting track-and-field events of the 1960 Olympics was the marathon. Abebe Bikila from Ethiopia ran barefoot through the streets of Rome to capture the first-ever gold medal for a black African.

Jesse worked a number of jobs during these years, and he lent his name to an annual youth track meet known as the ARCO/Jesse Owens Games. Young people age ten to fifteen competed in several events, and the games proved so popular that many other cities held their own version of the meet. The Jesse Owens Games continued for many years. For each event held, Jesse received a fee for the use of his name.

66The public has made you, even though you have won something on your own. . . . There are many times now when I don't feel like doing something . . . but the public is not interested in explanations. You got to smile. You must. The moment you begin to think you are an ordinary human being with ordinary human being rights, then the public does not want you any longer.99

—JESSE OWENS

In 1968 Jesse accepted an invitation to attend the Summer Olympics in Mexico City, Mexico. He was to be a guest of the Mexican government as well as a consultant for the U.S. Olympic Committee and a radio commentator. In the months leading up to the games, Jesse held athletic clinics across Central America. And once again, Jesse began to hear rumors of a possible U.S. boycott of the games.

The year 1968 was a troubled time for the United States. Protests and marches were spreading across the country. Some people opposed U.S. involvement in the Vietnam War. People of all races—especially African Americans—joined the civil rights movement, demanding the right to life, freedom, and equal treatment. Some black athletes wanted to boycott the games to protest their treatment back in the United States. They knew that without their participation, the United States would have trouble winning many of the events in Mexico City.

SOUTH AFRICA BANNED

Many African nations nearly boycotted the 1968 Olympics because they objected to the involvement of South African athletes. At the time, South Africans lived under a system of racist laws called apartheid. The laws separated black Africans from white Africans. In the end, the International Olympic Committee banned the South African team from taking part in the games.

In the end, the African American athletes decided to take part in the games. But their troubles weren't over—all of the Americans struggled to adjust to the city's altitude. Mexico City lies at an elevation of 7,000 feet, in a huge flat plain surrounded by mountains. Athletes not used to such conditions found themselves quickly winded in the thin, oxygen-poor air. But those used to the altitude, particularly runners from the highlands of Ethiopia and Kenya, took advantage of these conditions to win their races. U.S. athletes took gold medals in the 100-meter dash (Jim Hines), the 400-meter dash (Lee Evans), the 110-meter hurdles (Willie Davenport), and both the 100-meter and 400-meter relays. Bob Beamon won the long jump with an incredible jump of 29 feet, 2½ inches, and Dick Fosbury took the high jump with a leap of 7 feet, 4¼ inches and his famous backward "Fosbury flop," a style that changed the event forever.

Two African American sprinters, John Carlos and Tommie Smith, won the gold and bronze medals, respectively, in the 200-meter dash. But Carlos and Smith wanted to demonstrate their strong opinions against conditions in the United States. When they went to the medal stand for the playing of the national anthem, they raised their gloved fists and bowed their heads in protest as the music sounded through the stadium. This "black power" salute was a show of anger and disrespect for their home country, seen by millions of television viewers around the world.

After the medal ceremony, Jesse met with Carlos and Smith to ask them to apologize for their behavior. While Jesse was sympathetic to the concerns of the African American athletes, he didn't believe that the Olympic Games were the proper venue for protest. Carlos and Smith refused to listen. The next day, they were kicked off the U.S. team and sent home.

The meeting with Carlos and Smith left Jesse sad and bitter. In response, he worked with a writer to produce a book in which he described his own life and struggles with poverty and prejudice. Jesse named his book *Blackthink.* Jesse didn't believe that demonstrations and riots would effectively fight social wrongs. He felt that every person in the United States had the opportunity to get ahead in life. But when many young African Americans read Jesse's book, they didn't agree with his point of view. They thought that he was out of touch with the problems their generation faced.

Second thoughts on the subject of racism and life in the modern United States inspired Jesse to write another book, *I Have Changed.* In this book, he talked about his own problems and failings as an athlete, a businessman, and a family man. He showed sympathy for the problems of African Americans in the modern world, but he emphasized his belief that if a poor African American kid who had grown up in an Alabama shack could achieve success, then anyone anywhere could achieve it.

AWARDS AND HONORS

In 1972 Ohio State awarded Jesse an honorary doctorate in Athletic Arts. In 1974 the National Collegiate Athletic Association awarded him the Theodore Roosevelt Award, an honor for his activities in support of college athletics after the end of his track career. That year, he also became a member of the Track and Field Hall of Fame. In 1976 he received the Medal of Freedom, the country's highest civilian honor, from President Gerald Ford.

In 1972, the year *I Have Changed* came out, Jesse traveled to Munich, Germany, for the first Olympics held in that country since 1936. The Munich Olympics were meant to symbolize a Europe once again united after a century of war and strife. The star of the U.S. squad, swimmer Mark Spitz, won seven gold medals in individual and team events. The crowds cheered wildly for Spitz, who had movie-star looks and a brash personality. The support of the Munich fans for Spitz, a Jewish athlete, was a hopeful sign that Germany had left behind its anti-Semitic past.

But tragedy struck when a group of Palestinian terrorists burst into the Olympic Village, killing two athletes and taking nine others hostage. The athletes came from Israel, the Jewish state founded in the Middle East after World War II. Palestinians also lived in Israel and had lived there for centuries. Many Palestinians wanted the Israeli state returned to them. The terrorists staged the attack to call attention to their cause. The German police mounted a rescue attempt, but it failed and all of the Jewish hostages were killed. The world was horrified.

In a less-publicized incident, Jesse landed in another controversy. Two African Americans, Vincent Matthews and Wayne Collett, won gold and silver, respectively, in the 400-meter dash. Like Carlos and Smith in 1968, the two men wanted to show their displeasure at conditions for African Americans in the

United States. They crowded together on the top step of the podium, refused to stand at attention, and talked throughout the playing of the national anthem. Jesse tried to speak to them after the ceremony, but like Carlos and Smith, they refused to apologize. They were disqualified from any future Olympic competition.

Berlin, Germany, honored Jesse Owens by naming a street after him in 1984. Jesse Owens Allee runs near the Olympic Stadium, which still stands in the Charlottenburg district of western Berlin. There is also a Jesse Owens Realschule (high school) in Berlin.

Jesse still believed the Olympic Games should exemplify a spirit of friendly international competition, free from politics and protest. He was named to the board of directors of the U.S. Olympic Committee in 1973. He arranged for private companies to donate money to help Olympic athletes to support themselves while training. And Jesse never stopped moving and traveling. He gave speeches to civic and business groups on the values of hard work, patriotism, love of family, and, above all, hope for the future.

Keeping the Faith

As the 1970s drew to a close, Jesse was beginning to feel his age. Travels and speeches were tiring him, and he began to experience sudden coughing fits. A Chicago doctor diagnosed him with lung cancer—the result of a thirty-five-year cigarette habit. Jesse went through chemotherapy, but the illness didn't respond to treatment.

He lived out his last days in a home he and Ruth had purchased in Scottsdale, Arizona. Ruth and their three daughters remained at his side. Jesse Owens died on March 31, 1980. The state of Arizona honored Jesse by declaring a day of mourning and flying all flags at half-mast. People came from all over the country to pay their respects.

After a long life of energy and speed and of disappointment as well as accomplishment, Jesse Owens finally had come to rest. But he was not forgotten. Ohio State remembered him with the Jesse Owens Track and a Jesse Owens Memorial Plaza. The Jesse Owens Foundation offers scholarships to young athletes. In New York, a Jesse Owens Invitational track meet was held. Jesse's hometown of Oakville, Alabama, built a statue of him, showing Jesse dashing through the five rings that symbolize the Olympic Games. In 1990 President George H. W. Bush honored Ruth Owens with the Congressional Gold Medal, given in Jesse's name for his outstanding athletic achievements.

Many sportswriters consider Jesse Owens to be one of the finest athletes of the twentieth century. The sight of him hurtling down the track at Berlin, easily passing opponents and defying Adolf Hitler's racism, still inspires not only young athletes but people in much slower, more ordinary walks of life who are struggling to overcome barriers to their own hopes and dreams.

Near the end of his life, Jesse became friends with an athletic African American couple named Bill and Evelyn Lewis. They had a young son named Carl. When Carl was thirteen, he won a long jump competition and Jesse presented him with his award.

As a high school student, Carl began to dream of matching Jesse's amazing feat of winning four track-and-field gold medals in a single Olympics. In fact, he wanted to win gold in the same four events that Jesse had won. Carl's chance came in the 1984 Olympics in Los Angeles. That year Jesse Owens's granddaughter, Gina Hemphill, had the honor of carrying the Olympic torch into the stadium during the opening ceremony. Carl started off by winning gold in the 100 meters. In the next few days, he won the long jump and the 200 meters. Finally, Carl ran the anchor leg of the 4×100-meter relay. He finished off the relay in a blaze of speed, helping to set a new world-record time of 37.83 seconds. It had taken nearly fifty years since Jesse's wins in Berlin for another American to equal his achievement.

No doubt Jesse's legacy will endure as an inspiration to young athletes of all races. As Jesse himself said in the closing pages of his memoir *Jesse,* "I have always tried to do what my father vowed to do—the hardest thing. Always keep the faith."

PERSONAL STATISTICS

Name:

James Cleveland Owens

Nicknames:

J.C., Jesse, Buckeye Bullet

Born:

September 12, 1913

Died:

March 31, 1980

Height:

5'10"

Weight:

165 lbs.

TRACK-AND-FIELD RECORDS
SET BY JESSE OWENS

1928

High jump (junior high athletes): 6 feet, 0 inches

Broad jump (junior high athletes): 22 feet, 11¾ inches

1933

Broad jump (high school athletes): 24 feet, 9⅝ inches

220-yard dash (high school athletes): 20.7 seconds

100-yard dash (high school athletes record and world record tie): 9.4 seconds

1934

Broad jump (Ohio State athletes): 23 feet, 10¾ inches

90-yard dash (world): 8.6 seconds

120-yard dash (world): 11.5 seconds

1935

220-yard dash (world): 20.3 seconds

Broad jump (world): 26 feet, 8¼ inches

220-yard low hurdles (world): 22.6 seconds

Indoor 60-meter dash (world): 6.6 seconds

1936

        100-yard dash (world): 9.3 seconds

        200-meter dash (world): 21.1 seconds

        4×100-meter relay (world): 39.8 seconds

1936 Olympic Games, Berlin

        100-meter dash: 10.3 seconds (gold)

        200-meter dash: 20.7 seconds (gold)

        Broad jump: 26 feet, 5¼ inches (gold)

        4×100-meter relay: 39.8 seconds (gold)

SOURCES

7   William J. Baker, *Jesse Owens: An American Life* (New York, Free Press, 1986), 11.

9   Baker, *Jesse Owens*, 11.

9–10   Jesse Owens with Paul Niemark, *Jesse: A Spiritual Autobiography* (Plainfield, NJ: Logos International, 1978), 35.

11   Baker, *Jesse Owens*, 9–10.

14   Jesse Owens and Paul Neimark. *Blackthink: My Life as Black Man and White Man* (New York: Pocket Books, 1971), 125.

15   Bill Libby, *Stars of the Olympics* (New York: Hawthorn Books, Inc., 1975), 66.

16   Owens, *Jesse*, 138.

21   Ibid., 45.

25   Baker, *Jesse Owens*, 31.

36   Ibid., 23.

37   Associated Press, "Owens Surpasses 3 World Records," *New York Times*, May 26, 1935, S1.

42   Baker, *Jesse Owens*, 55.

43   "Brundage Favors Berlin Olympics," *New York Times*, July 27, 1935, 2.

44   "FAQs," *International Olympic Committee*, n.d., http://www. olympic.org/uk/utilities/faq_detail _uk.asp?rdo_cat=10_39_0 (March 24, 2005).

47   Jesse Owens and Paul Neimark, *Jesse: The Man Who Outran Hitler* (Plainfield, NJ: Logos International, 1978), 28.

55   Baker, *Jesse Owens*, 92.

56   Daley, Arthur J., "Owens Captures Olympic Titles, Equals World 100-Meter Record," *New York Times*, August 4, 1936, 1.

68   Baker, *Jesse Owens*, 113.

68   "Gov. Davey of Ohio Cables Felicitations to Owens," *New York Times*, August 5, 1936, 27.

70   Libby, *Stars of the Olympics*, 68.

80   Baker, *Jesse Owens*, 47.

81   Owens, *Jesse*, 122.

84   "Owens, 'Jesse' (James C.)," *HickockSports.com*, September 9, 2004, http://www.hickoksports .com/biograph/owensjesse.shtml (January 26, 2005).

86   Owens, *Jesse*, 136.

90   Baker, *Jesse Owens*, 183.

98   Owens, *Jesse*, 201.

BIBLIOGRAPHY

Baker, William J. *Jesse Owens: An American Life.* New York: Free Press, 1986.

Entine, John, and Earl Smith. *Taboo: Why Black Athletes Dominate Sports and Why We're Afraid to Talk About It.* New York: PublicAffairs, 2000.

Killanin, Lord, and John Rodda. *The Olympic Games: 80 Years of People, Events and Records.* New York: Macmillan, 1976.

Mandell, Richard D. *The Nazi Olympics.* New York: Macmillan, 1971.

McRae, Donald. *Heroes Without a Country: America's Betrayal of Joe Louis and Jesse Owens.* New York: Ecco, 2002.

Owens, Jesse, with Paul G. Niemark. *Blackthink: My Life as a Black Man and White Man.* New York: Morrow, 1970.

Owens, Jesse, with Paul G. Niemark. *I Have Changed.* New York: Morrow, 1972.

Owens, Jesse, with Paul Niemark. *Jesse: A Spiritual Autobiography.* Plainfield, NJ: Logos International, 1978.

Owens, Jesse, with Paul G. Niemark. *The Jesse Owens Story.* New York: Putnam, 1970.

WEBSITES

The Ancient Olympics

www.perseus.tufts.edu/Olympics/

This site features articles about ancient and modern Olympic athletes, a tour of ancient Olympia, and information on the history of the games.

Jesse Owens Museum

www.jesseowensmuseum.org

The Jesse Owens Museum in Danville, Alabama, has a site that incorporates a museum tour, a kids' quiz, and useful links to newspaper and magazine articles on Jesse Owens.

The Official Jesse Owens Website

www.jesseowens.com

This site includes a biography, a list of achievements, photos, quotes, and links.

Owens Pierced a Myth

espn.go.com/sportscentury/features/00016393.html

This article on Jesse Owens's Olympic performance is part of the ESPN website, which named Jesse Owens as sixth in its list of the one hundred greatest athletes of the twentieth century.

INDEX

A
Adidas, 54
African American athletes,
    44, 48, 55, 61, 70–
    71, 81, 83, 90–94
    Carlos, John, 92
    Collett, Wayne, 94
    Gordon, Ed, 27
    Gourdin, Ned, 18
    Hubbard, William
    DeHart, 18
    Johnson, Cornelius, 53
    Lewis, Carl, 97–98
    Matthews, Vincent, 94
    Metcalfe, Ralphe, 26–
    27, 30, 47–48, 55–
    56, 62–64
    Smith, Tommie, 92
    Tolan, Eddie, 26–27,
    48, 61
Albritton, Dave, 55
All American Track and
    Field team, 35
Amateur Athletic Union
    (AAU), 35, 41–42,
    45, 66–68, 73, 75
    Sullivan Trophy, 73
apartheid, 91
ARCO/Jesse Owens Games,
    89

B
Baillet-Latour, Henri de, 53
Beamon, Bob, 92
Bikila, Abebe, 89
Blackthink, 92
Bolton Elementary, 8–9
Boston, Ralph, 89
Brundage, Avery, 43–45
Buckeye Bullet, 56
Bush, George H. W., 97

C
Cantor, Eddie, 70
Carlos, John, 92
Cincinnati Crescents, 82
civil rights movement, 90
Clotworthy, Bob, 32
Cold War, 85, 87
Collett, Wayne, 94

Consolidated Artists, 73–74
Cromwell, Dean, 39, 52

D
Dassler, Adolph "Adi," 54
Davenport, Willie, 91
Davey, Martin L., 68
Davis, Glenn, 32
Dillard, Harrison, 85
discrimination, 33, 35, 69,
    92–93
Draper, Foy, 62–63
Duffey, Dan, 41

E
East Technical High School,
    1–3, 23–25, 28, 30–31
Eisenhower, Dwight, 87
Evans, Lee, 91

F
Fairmount Junior High
    School, 9, 14, 20
Fleischer, Tilly, 53
Ford, Gerald, 93
Ford Motor Company,
    81–82
Forkins, Marty, 70–73
Fosbury, Dick, 92

G
Glickman, Marty, 62–64
Goodwill Ambassador, 85
Gordon, Ed, 27
Gourdin, Ned, 18

H
Harlem Globetrotters, 74,
    82
Harrison, William Henry, 31
Hemphill, Gina, 97
Hindenburg, 52–53
Hines, Jim, 91
Hitler, Adolph, 42–43, 50,
    52–53, 63, 66, 69, 78,
    97
Hohlmayer, Alice "Lefty," 32
Hubbard, William DeHart,
    18

I
I Have Changed, 93
Illinois Youth Commission,
    86

J
Jesse, 98
Jessie Owens Allee, 95
Jessie Owens Dry Cleaning
    Company, 76
Jessie Owens Foundation,
    97
Jesse Owens Games, 89
Jessie Owens Invitational,
    97
Jessie Owens Memorial
    Plaza, 97
Jessie Owens Realschule,
    95
Jessie Owens Track, 97
Johnson, Cornelius, 53

K
Konno, Ford, 32
Kroesen, Richard, 32–33

L
Landon, Alf, 70–71
Lewis, Bill, 97
Lewis, Carl, 97–98
Lewis, Evelyn, 97
Locke, Roland, 38
Long, Luz, 59–60

M
marathon, 13
Matthews, Vincent, 94
McCaw, Julio, 72
McDaniel, Mildred, 88
Medal of Freedom, 93
Metcalfe, Ralphe, 26–27, 30,
    47–48, 55–56, 62–64
Morris, Glenn, 73
Morrow, Bobby, 88
Murphy, Michael, 13

N
National Collegiate Athletic
    Association
    Championships, 39

National Collegiate Athletic Association Theodore Roosevelt Award, 93
National Collegiate Track and Field Championships, 36–38
National Interscholastic Championship, 1–3
Nazi party, 42–44, 50, 52
Nicklaus, Jack, 32
Nurmi, Paavo, 65

O
Office of Civilian Defense, 80–81
Ohio State, 30–36, 39, 42, 79–80, 93, 96
Olympians, 74–77
Olympic Games, 13, 19–23, 25–27, 32, 36, 40–66, 69, 78, 82, 84, 87–92, 94–95, 97–98
Olympics (softball team), 76
Osendarp, Martin, 56
Outlin, Cliff, 88
Owens, Beverly, 74
Owens, Gloria Shirley, 27, 31
Owens, Henry, 4–7, 22, 80
Owens, James Cleveland "Jesse"
    All American Track and Field team, 35
    bankruptcy, 77
    books by, 92–93, 98
    childhood, 4–14
    college running, 32–48
    early running, 13–20
    Goodwill Ambassador, 85
    high school, 1–3, 23–32
    Illinois Youth Commission, 86
    junior high school, 9, 14, 20
    marriage, 40
    Medal of Freedom, 93
    Olympic gold medals, 57, 60, 61, 64
    Personal Stats, 99
    Track and Field Hall of Fame, 93
    records, 100–101

Owens, Lillie, 7
Owens, Marlene, 77
Owens, Mary Emma Fitzgerald, 5–7
Owens, Ruth Solomon, 27–28, 31–32, 40, 73–74, 96-97

P
Paddock, Charley, 19–20, 36, 85
Parsley, Lea Ann, 32
Peacock, Eulace, 39–40, 45–48
Pearl Harbor, 80
Penn Relays, 46–47
Puma, 54

R
Republican Party, 70
Riley, Charles, 2, 9, 10–12, 14–15, 17–20, 22, 24, 28, 30, 36, 38, 73
Ritola, Ville, 65
Robertson, Lawson, 55, 62–63
Robinson, Bill "Bojangles," 70–71
Robinson, Elizabeth, 23
Robinson, Jackie, 61
Robinson, Mack, 60–61
Rodriques, Conrado, 72
Roosevelt, Franklin D., 69

S
Smith, Tommie, 92
Snyder, Larry, 34, 36, 42, 52, 55, 67, 79
Spitz, Mark, 94
Stagg Field, 1–2, 26, 29, 37
stock market crash, 22
Stoller, Sam, 62–64
Sullivan Trophy, 73

T
Theodore Roosevelt Award, 93
Tolan, Eddie, 26–27, 48, 61
Track and Field Hall of Fame, 93

V
Vietnam War, 90

W
Weil, Edgar, 24, 28
White, Willye, 88
Whitlock, Harold, 60
Woellke, Hans, 53
World War II, 78, 81–82
    Pearl Harbor, 80
Wykoff, Frank, 55, 62, 64